A CourseGuide for

Know the Creeds and Councils

Justin Holcomb

ZONDERVAN ACADEMIC

A CourseGuide for Know the Creeds and Councils
Copyright © 2020 by Zondervan

Requests for information should be addressed to:
Zondervan, *3900 Sparks Dr. SE, Grand Rapids, Michigan 49546*

ISBN 978-0-310-11094-1 (softcover)

Printed in the United States of America

CONTENTS

Introduction

Welcome to *A CourseGuide for Know the Creeds and Councils*. These guides were created for formal and informal students alike who want to engage deeper in biblical, theological, or ministry studies. We hope this guide will provide an opportunity for you to grow not only in your understanding, but also in your faith.

How to Use This Guide

This guide is meant to be used in conjunction with the book *Know the Creeds and Councils* and its corresponding videos, *Know the Creeds and Councils Video Lectures*. After you have read each chapter in the book and watched the accompanying video lesson, the materials in this guide will help you review and assess what you have learned. Application-oriented questions are included as well. For additional practice, you will want to complete exercises found in *Know the Creeds and Councils Workbook*.

Each CourseGuide has been individually designed to best equip you in your studies, but in general, you can expect the following components. Most CourseGuides begin every chapter with a "You Should Know" section, which highlights key terminology, people, and facts to remember. This section serves as a helpful summary for directing your studies. Reflection questions, typically two to three per chapter, prompt you to summarize key points you've learned. Discussion questions invite you to an even deeper level of engagement. Finally, most chapters will end with a short quiz to test your retention. You can find the answer key to each quiz at the bottom of the page following it.

For Further Study

CourseGuides accompany books and videos from some of the world's
top biblical and theological scholars. They may be used independently,
or in small groups or classrooms, offering quality instruction to
equip students for academic and ministry pursuits. If you would like
to engage in further study with Zondervan's CourseGuides, the full
lineup may be viewed online. After completing your studies with *A
CourseGuide for Know the Creeds and Councils*, we recommend moving
on to *A CourseGuide for How to Read the Bible for All Its Worth* and *A
CourseGuide for Introduction to Biblical Interpretation*.

CHAPTER 1

Apostles' Creed
(ca. 140)

You Should Know

- The Apostles' Creed is helpful to modern Christians for rooting the supernatural faith in historical realities.

- The legend behind why the Apostles' Creed is called the *Apostles'* Creed is that each of the twelve apostles was supposed to have contributed an article to the creed.

- The current Apostles' Creed was probably not compiled until the fifth century.

- Church historian Philip Schaff notes that the Apostles' Creed is the Creed of Creeds.

- The Apostles' Creed is helpful to modern Christians for rooting the supernatural faith in historical realities.

- The Apostles' Creed directs believers toward life everlasting.

- Descent into hell: Old Testament imagery; it meant that Christ actually died

- Holy catholic church: the church's existence wherever in the world the gospel is preached

- Old Roman Creed: used during baptisms in early Christendom, its basic tenets were used in the Apostles' Creed

Essay Questions

Short

1. How can the Apostles' Creed be considered the "Creed of Creeds"?

2. According to Holcomb, there is no *explicit* doctrine of the Trinity in the Apostles' Creed. Does the creed lead one to conclude that God is Triune, and does it provide a foundation for further study?

3. What are some ways the Apostles' Creed can be utilized in your local church?

Long

1. Explain each of the twelve articles of the Apostles' Creed as if someone asked you what each of them meant. What Scriptures would you use?

Quiz

1. What is the legend behind why the Apostles' Creed is called the *Apostles'* Creed?

  a) Each of the twelve apostles was supposed to have contributed an article to the creed.

  b) Peter was rumored to have written half of the creed and Paul the other half.

  c) The apostolic church fathers came together to compose a summary of the New Testament.

  d) The creed was a relic found in a monastery said to house the bones of most of the apostles.

2. What creed did the Apostles' Creed develop from?

  a) The Old Roman Creed

  b) The Nicene Creed

  c) The Old Asian Creed

  d) The Disciple's Creed

3. The current Apostles' Creed was probably not compiled until the:

    a) Second century
    b) Fifth century
    c) Sixth century
    d) Third century

4. Which Protestant church still recites the Apostles' Creed during morning and evening prayer?

    a) Every Protestant church
    b) The Moravian church
    c) The Church of England
    d) The Scottish Presbyterian church

5. Church historian Philip Schaff notes that the Apostles' Creed is:

    a) Antiquated
    b) The only creed that matters
    c) The prayer of prayers
    d) The Creed of Creeds

6. Which of the following is a doctrine the Apostles' Creed does not contain?

    a) The relationship of Christ to God
    b) The incarnation of Christ
    c) The forgiveness of sins
    d) The resurrection of the dead

7. Which of the following is a doctrine the Apostles' Creed does contain?

    a) The identity of the Holy Spirit
    b) The relationship of Christ to God
    c) The story of the Gospels
    d) The doctrine of the Trinity

8. "He descended into hell" most likely meant what to early Christians?

    a) It teaches that Christ preached the gospel for three days to Old Testament saints after he died.
    b) Using Old Testament imagery, it meant that Christ actually died.

c) That phrase was not in the original Apostles' Creed.

d) It is an allusion to Christ preaching through Noah during the days prior to the Genesis flood.

9. In the Apostles' Creed, what is "the holy catholic church" a reference to?

a) The church wherever religious people live

b) The church before the Eastern and Western churches split

c) The Roman Catholic Church

d) The church's existence wherever in the world the gospel is preached

10. The Apostles' Creed is helpful to modern Christians for:

a) Rooting the supernatural faith in historical realities

b) Showing that Christianity is similar to other faiths

c) Describing ancient history

d) Providing a comprehensive confession of Christian doctrine

CHAPTER 2

Council of Nicaea and the Nicene Creed (325)

You Should Know

- The heart of the issue at Nicaea was how Christians can worship the Father and worship Jesus and still claim to worship one true God.

- Alexander's argument for the Son being God was that the Father cannot change, so he must eternally be a Father to the Son.

- Arius: the presbyter who sparked the controversy of Nicaea with his controversial views on the nature of the Son

- Athanasius: wrote *On the Incarnation* defending the one *homoousios* of the Father and Son

- *Homoousios*: Greek word meaning "one substance"

- *Monogenous*: Greek word meaning "only-begotten"

- Origen: Church father who taught that the Father was due glory and reverence as God himself that was not due to the Son

- Constantine: the emperor who called the Council of Nicaea

- Council of Constantinople: convened in AD 381

- Council of Nicaea: convened in AD 325

Essay Questions

Short

1. What was wrong in Arius' reasoning concerning how he saw the relationship between the Father and the Son? How did Alexander counter Arius' views about the Son?

2. What does it mean for the Nicene Creed to describe the "minimum" of Christian belief? (p. 38)

3. What was at stake if the Council of Nicaea had not ruled against Arius? (p. 38–39)

Long

1. What Scripture proofs would you use to defend each of the Nicene Creed's doctrines? Explain why.

Quiz

1. Which emperor called the Council of Nicaea?
    a) Constans
    b) Augustus
    c) Theodosius
    d) Constantine

2. Who was the presbyter that sparked the controversy of Nicaea with his controversial views on the nature of the Son?
    a) Eusebius
    b) Origen
    c) Arius
    d) Athanasius

3. Which church father taught that the Father was due glory and reverence as God himself that was not due to the Son?
    a) Athanasius
    b) Clement
    c) Irenaeus
    d) Origen

4. What was Alexander's argument for the Son being God?
    a) The Father cannot change, so he must eternally be a Father to the Son.
    b) The Father created the Son and adopted him.

    c) The Father and the Spirit together made the Son as the first-born of creation.

    d) The Father becomes the Father at Jesus's baptism by John.

5. The heart of the issue at Nicaea was:

    a) Which books of the New Testament should be included?

    b) How can bishops be encouraged to remain at their churches?

    c) How can Christians worship the Father and worship Jesus and still claim to worship one true God?

    d) How can Christians confess the Holy Spirit as Lord?

6. The Nicene Creed follows the basic model of what other creed?

    a) The Apostles' Creed

    b) The Athanasian Creed

    c) The Chalcedonian Creed

    d) The Ten Commandments

7. The Nicene Creed calls Jesus _____ or _____.

    a) *Monogenous*, only unique

    b) *Monogenous*, only-begotten

    c) *Monophysite*, eternally subordinate

    d) *Monothelite*, one man

8. The orthodox theologians at Nicaea added which phrase to finally counter their opponents?

    a) "Of two substances"

    b) "Of similar substance"

    c) "Of one substance"

    d) "Of similar essence"

9. The doctrine of the Holy Spirit in the Nicene Creed was expanded by which council?

    a) The First Council of Constantinople

    b) The Council of Ephesus

    c) The Second Council of Constantinople

    d) The Council of Chalcedon

10. Athanasius wrote which book defending the one *homoousios* of the Father and Son?

    a) *On the Incarnation*
    b) *Against Heresies*
    c) *On the Unity of Christ*
    d) *On the Only-Begotten Son*

CHAPTER 3

Councils of Ephesus (431, 449, 475)

You Should Know

- The doctrine of divine impassibility is that God is not controlled by emotions.

- Cyril feared that Nestorius's views would ultimately separate the two natures of Christ.

- Nestorius's Christology was an attempt to counter Arianism and Manicheanism.

- Nestorian missionaries established churches in Iran, India, and China.

- *Theotokos*: Greek word meaning "Mother of God"; a title ascribed to Mary, asserting that she bore God in her womb

- Theodosius II: Roman emperor who convened the Council of Ephesus

- The Twelve Anathemas: Cyril's proactive letter condemning Nestorius and anyone who did not affirm Cyril's twelve points about Christ

- Cyril: the patriarch of Alexandria; emphasized the unity of Christ's two natures in the one person; strongly affirmed Jesus's divinity

- Nestorius: the patriarch of Constantinople; emphasized the distinct natures of Christ and feared confusing them; strongly affirmed Jesus's humanity

- Council of Ephesus: AD 431, the First Council of Ephesus

Essay Questions

Short

1. Why is it important to know how, in so far as we are capable of understanding it, Christ is both human and divine? Why is it important to affirm both aspects of Christ for his work of atonement?

2. Why would Cyril fear that Nestorius's view would lead to believing Jesus was two people loosely tied together? Do you think this was a legitimate fear?

3. Why would Nestorius view Cyril's theology as leading to a God who absorbed the humanity of Christ into divinity? Do you think this was a legitimate fear?

Long

1. Explain the doctrines Cyril and Nestorius were respectively trying to uphold and how they were seeking to maintain them. Why do you think the church theologically accepted Cyril's view over Nestorius's? Would you have seen the unity of Christ's natures as that important of an issue if you were there?

Quiz

1. What year was the ecumenical Council of Ephesus held?
    a) AD 475
    b) AD 449
    c) AD 431
    d) AD 428

2. Which council of Ephesus is considered ecumenical?
    a) The First Council
    b) The Second Council
    c) The Third Council
    d) None of these councils are considered ecumenical.

3. The Patriarch of Constantinople during the events of the Council of Ephesus was:

   a) Nestorius
   b) Celestine
   c) Cyril
   d) Athanasius

4. The Patriarch of Alexandria during the events of the Council of Ephesus was:

   a) Nestorius
   b) Celestine
   c) Cyril
   d) Athanasius

5. The doctrine of divine impassibility is:

   a) God is ruled by emotion.
   b) God cannot become man.
   c) God has no emotions.
   d) God is not controlled by emotions.

6. Nestorius's Christology was an attempt to counter _____ and _____.

   a) Apollinarianism, Platonism
   b) Gnosticism, atheism
   c) Nicaea, Ephesus
   d) Arianism, Manichaeanism

7. According to Holcomb, Nestorius emphasized Jesus's:

   a) Sonship
   b) Divinity
   c) Humanity
   d) Death

8. According to Holcomb, Cyril emphasized Jesus's:

   a) Sonship
   b) Divinity
   c) Humanity
   d) Death

9. The phrase that was the catalyst to creating conflict between Cyril and Nestorius was:

   a) *Homoousios*, or same substance
   b) *Theotokos*, or Mother of God
   c) *Anthropos*, or man
   d) *Christotokos*, or Mother of Christ

10. Cyril feared that Nestorius's views would ultimately:

   a) Separate the two natures of Christ
   b) Lead to Arianism
   c) Teach the people to call Mary the mother of God
   d) Merge the two natures of Christ into one

CHAPTER 4

Council of Chalcedon (451)

You Should Know

- The statement in the Chalcedonian Definition "Without any confusion, change, division or separation" excludes both Eutychianism and Nestorianism.

- Jesus Christ is two in natures and one in person.

- Chalcedon affirmed that Christ is of one substance with the Father according to his divinity and of one substance with us according to his humanity.

- Leo was the Pope of Rome who wrote a tome condemning Eutyches.

- *Anhypostasia/enhypostasia*: Christ's human nature did not exist as a person without the divine person of the *Logos* to assume it. (p. 57)

- Council of Chalcedon: convened in AD 451

- Eutyches: emphasized the union of the two natures of Christ into one nature

- Monophysitism: the view that Christ's two natures merged into a new "third nature," neither divine nor human

- The communication of properties: doctrine that allows one to attribute properties of both natures to the one person while allowing each nature to retain its own attributes

- The Definition of Chalcedon was written from extrabiblical ideas to describe the person of Jesus; not really a definition, but rather a set of boundaries; a statement of the mystery of faith delivered to us by the prophets and Christ; and a way to correct our extremes of thinking.

Essay Questions

Short

1. What was the teaching of Eutyches? Why did the church oppose his view?

2. What are Cyril's doctrinal contributions to the Definition of Chalcedon?

3. How does the statement "without any confusion, change, division or separation" preserve our understanding of Christ's two natures in one person? Why is it important to understand the distinction between *nature* and *person* when discussing these issues?

Long

1. How does *Theotokos*, *homoousios*, and *anhypostasia/enhypostasia* contribute to our understanding of the doctrine of the incarnation? How would you explain these terms to an ordinary person in the pew, and why they are important?

Quiz

1. _____ emphasized the union of the two natures of Christ into one nature.

    a) Leo

    b) Cyril

    c) Eutyches

    d) Eusebius

2. _____ is the view that Christ's two natures merged into a new "third nature," neither divine nor human.

    a) Monophysitism

    b) Nestorianism

    c) Monothelitism

    d) Cyrillianism

3. What year did the Council of Chalcedon convene?

   a) AD 420
   b) AD 472
   c) AD 431
   d) AD 451

4. Which pope sent his "Tome" to the Council of Chalcedon to express his views on Christology?

   a) Eutyches
   b) Celestine
   c) Leo
   d) Cyril

5. What theological works were consulted by the Council of Chalcedon?

   a) The Nicene Creed
   b) The letter from Cyril to Nestorius
   c) The Tome of Leo
   d) All of the above

6. Chalcedon affirmed that Christ is _____ with the Father according to his divinity and _____ with us according to his humanity.

   a) Of two substances, of one substance
   b) Of one substance, of one substance
   c) Of a similar substance, of two substances
   d) Of a different substance, of a similar substance

7. What statement in the Chalcedonian Definition excludes both Eutychianism and Nestorianism?

   a) Without change or confusion, but division and separation
   b) Without any confusion, change, division, or separation
   c) Without separation or division, but change and merging
   d) None of the above

8. Jesus Christ is _____ in nature(s) and _____ in person(s).

   a) One, one
   b) One, two
   c) Two, one
   d) Two, two

9. What is the *anhypostasia/enhypostasia* distinction?

   a) Christ's human nature did not exist as a person without the divine person of the *Logos* to assume it.
   b) Christ's human nature existed as a person prior to the divine person of the *Logos* assuming it.
   c) Christ has two *hypostases* which merge into one *hypostasis* afterward.
   d) Christ's divine nature, the *Logos*, only became an individual person after assuming a human nature.

10. What doctrine allows one to attribute properties of both natures to the one person while allowing each nature to retain its own attributes?

   a) The Trinity
   b) Christology
   c) The communication of properties
   d) The communication of the Spirit

CHAPTER 5

Athanasian Creed (Late 400s to Early 500s)

You Should Know

- We do not know who wrote the Athanasian Creed.

- Athanasius led in the defense of the faith of Nicaea by claiming the Father and Son are the very same substance.

- Augustine was a great Western church father who wrote *On the Trinity*.

- Athanasius led in the defense of the faith of Nicaea by claiming the Father and Son are the very same substance.

- Mutability is not a quality of divinity.

- The Greek church rejected the Athanasian Creed.

- Modalism: the view that God chooses to appear as different persons of the Trinity at different times

- Neo-Arianism: the view that the Father is to be regarded as more God than the Son and Holy Spirit even though they are all God

- Aseity: God as he is to himself

- Anathema: list of beliefs rendered unacceptable to Christian conviction by the truths expressed in the creed they are found in

Essay Questions

Short

1. Summarize the Athanasian Creed's doctrines of the Trinity and the two natures of Christ.

2. What is Neo-Arianism, and how does the Athanasian Creed counter it?

3. What is Modalism, and how does the Athanasian Creed counter it?

Long

1. Based on your current understanding and readings, explain the biblical doctrines of the Trinity and the two natures, one personhood of Christ while being faithful to the creedal boundaries that have been presented so far.

Quiz

1. Athanasius led in the defense of the faith of Nicaea by claiming:
    a) The Father and Son are differentiated as Creator and creature.
    b) The Son is eternally subordinate to the Father.
    c) The Father and Son are of a very similar substance.
    d) The Father and Son are the very same substance.

2. The Athanasian Creed shows reliance upon the thought of:
    a) Aquinas
    b) Boethius
    c) Arius
    d) Augustine

3. What medieval theologian counted the Athanasian Creed, the Apostles' Creed, and the Nicene Creed as the *Tria Symbola*, or Three Creeds of the Christian faith?
    a) Martin Luther
    b) Aquinas
    c) Anselm
    d) Augustine

4. Which work does the Athanasian Creed quote verbatim at points?
    a) Cyril's *First Letter to Nestorius*
    b) Augustine's *On the Trinity*
    c) Athanasius' *On the Incarnation*
    d) Basil's *On the Holy Spirit*

5. What does "aseity" mean?
   a) God as he is to himself
   b) God as we understand him
   c) God's knowledge of creatures
   d) A technical term for the incarnation

6. Holcomb notes the Athanasian Creed is essentially:
   a) A textbook about God
   b) A map to understanding ourselves
   c) A document that creates more problems than it solves
   d) A guide to worship

7. Which is not a quality of divinity?
   a) Uncreated
   b) Mutability
   c) Unlimited
   d) Eternal

8. What is the view that the Father is to be regarded as more God than the Son and Holy Spirit even though they are all God?
   a) Nicene Orthodoxy
   b) Gnosticism
   c) Neo-Arianism
   d) Cyrillianism

9. What is the view that God chooses to appear as different persons of the Trinity at different times?
   a) Nicene Orthodoxy
   b) Modalism
   c) Arianism
   d) Apollinarianism

10. According to Holcomb, believing in the God whom the creeds testify to is a matter of:
   a) Historical interest
   b) Little importance
   c) Salvation
   d) None of the above

ANSWER KEY

1. D, 2. D, 3. C, 4. B, 5. A, 6. D, 7. B, 8. C, 9. B, 10. C

CHAPTER 6

Councils of Constantinople (381, 553, 681)

You Should Know

- Christ needed to possess a human will in addition to his divine will in order that he might be fully human.

- For a few decades after Nicaea, Roman emperors tended to favor a form of Arianism.

- Constantinople II was convened to respond to the Monophysites.

- Gregory of Nazianzus was vital in defending the personhood of the Holy Spirit at the First Council of Constantinople.

- Constantinople: founded by Constantine; had three ecumenical councils meet there in AD 381, 553, 681

- Monothelitism: Christ has only one active will

- Dyothelite: Christ has two active wills since he has two natures

- Maximus the Confessor: theologian who defended a Dyothelite view of Christ's wills

- Semi-Arians: denied the personhood of the Holy Spirit

- Theodosius I: Roman emperor who convened the First Council of Constantinople

Essay Questions

Short

1. Why did the orthodox church fathers demand that faith acknowledge the Holy Spirit as a person of the Trinity rather than merely a power or force? Why would many in the church think the Holy Spirit was only a force or power?

2. What is Monothelitism? Who were its main adherents, and do you agree with it? Why or why not?

3. What is Dyothelitism? Who were its main adherents, and do you agree with it? Why or why not?

Long

1. What Scriptures can you think of that suggest the Holy Spirit is personal and not a force? In addition to guiding us to God, what other roles does the Holy Spirit play? What Scriptures aid us in understanding his work?

Quiz

1. Constantinople was founded by the Christian emperor:
   a) Constantine
   b) Constans
   c) Constantius
   d) Theodosius

2. How many ecumenical councils met at Constantinople?
   a) One
   b) Two
   c) Three
   d) Four

3. The First Council of Constantinople took place in:
   a) AD 325
   b) AD 381

c) AD 553

d) AD 681

4. For a few decades after Nicaea, Roman emperors tended to favor a form of:

a) Orthodoxy

b) Arianism

c) Paganism

d) Judaism

5. Which theologian was vital in defending the personhood of the Holy Spirit at the First Council of Constantinople?

a) Basil the Great

b) Gregory of Nyssa

c) Gregory of Nazianzus

d) Maximus the Confessor

6. Which emperor convened the First Council of Constantinople?

a) Constantine

b) Valens

c) Constantius

d) Theodosius

7. Constantinople II was convened to respond to whom?

a) The Monophysites

b) The Nestorians

c) The Arians

d) The Romans

8. Monothelitism is the belief that:

a) Christ was one messiah to the church.

b) Christ has only one will.

c) Christ has only one active will.

d) The Holy Spirit is a force.

9. The theologian who defended the Dyothelite position was:

a) Maximus

b) Sergius

c) Heraclius

d) Gregory of Rome

10. Christ needed to possess a human will in addition to his divine will in order that:

a) He might pretend to pray to God in order to teach us to pray.

b) He might be fully human.

c) He might unify the two natures into one.

d) None of the above

CHAPTER 7

Councils of Carthage and Orange (419 and 529)

You Should Know

- For Pelagius, humans could overcome their sin and fully eradicate evil from themselves.

- Augustine believed fallen humans were *non posse non peccare*, or not able not to sin.

- Adam's fall and humankind's sin directly confronts humans with the question of how responsible we are for our actions.

- Pelagius was opposed to the doctrine of original sin.

- Caelestius: Pelagius's disciple who spread his views in North Africa

- Donatists: A sect that believed the church should consist only of those who live perfectly holy lives

- Council of Carthage: council which upheld Augustine's views of grace and human sin over against Pelagius

- Pelagius: believed that humans had full freedom and full responsibility for their actions in choosing good or bad, however they pleased

- Augustine: believed that humans are born into the bondage of sin and only sin more and more unless God intervenes and gradually frees them to do good by the power of God's Spirit

- Theological anthropology: a description of humanity derived from a God-centered worldview

Essay Questions

Short

1. How did Pelagius's personal experiences influence his theology? (p. 87–88)

2. How does Augustine's doctrine of original sin shape his theology? (p. 89–91)

3. If Christ is a divine guide, what purpose might the crucifixion have for Pelagius?

Long

1. Based on Holcomb's presentation, do you agree with Augustine's theology? Why or why not? How would you counter or refute Pelagius?

Quiz

1. What is "theological anthropology?" (p. 85)
   a) A description of God derived from a God-centered worldview
   b) A description of humanity derived from a God-centered worldview
   c) A description of God derived from a human-centered worldview
   d) A description of humanity derived from a human-centered worldview

2. Adam's fall and humankind's sin directly confronts humans with the question of: (p. 86)
   a) Did Adam's sin cause the fall?
   b) How many generations from Adam do we descend?
   c) How responsible are we for our actions?
   d) None of the above

3. Who believed that humans had full freedom and full responsibility for their actions in choosing good or bad, however they pleased? (p. 86)
   a) Pelagius
   b) Augustine

c) Jerome

d) Tertullian

4. Who believed that humans are born into the bondage of sin and only sin more and more unless God intervenes and gradually frees them to do good by the power of God's Spirit? (p. 86)

a) Pelagius

b) Augustine

c) Jerome

d) Tertullian

5. The Council of _____ affirmed that Augustine's view was correct over against Pelagius. (p. 86–87)

a) Orange

b) Nicaea II

c) Ephesus

d) Carthage

6. For Pelagius, humans could: (p. 88)

a) Never be rid of sin in this life

b) Overcome their sin and fully eradicate evil from themselves

c) Become angels after reaching an estate of enlightenment

d) Become messiahs for one another

7. What doctrine was Pelagius opposed to? (p. 88)

a) Original sin

b) The deity of Christ

c) Inherent righteousness

d) The personhood of the Spirit

8. According to Holcomb, the _____ believed the church should consist only of those who live perfectly holy lives. (p. 88)

a) Arians

b) Manicheans

c) Donatists

d) Docetists

9. Augustine believed fallen humans were: (p. 89)

   a) *Posse non peccare et posse peccare*, or having both the power not to sin and the power to sin
   b) *Posse non peccare*, or able not to sin
   c) *Non posse non peccare*, or not able not to sin
   d) *Non posse peccare*, or unable to sin

10. Pelagius's disciple who spread his views in North Africa was: (p. 90)

    a) Augustine
    b) Caiaphas
    c) Caelestius
    d) Basil

CHAPTER 8

Council of Trent
(1545–63)

You Should Know

- Trent's doctrine of justification believed God is the one who justifies, justification is not a one-time event but a life-long work of transformation, and a believer cannot be assured of salvation in this life.

- v•The Roman Catholic sacrament of penance meant that a person had to confess his sins to a priest and do a work of satisfaction.

- Martin Luther sparked the Reformation by his opposition to indulgences in 1517, which eventually grew into a larger protest.

- Martin Luther advocated that we become justified through the imputed righteousness of Christ.

- Trent argued deceased saints could be prayed to because Christ has one body.

- Trent did not heal the fracture between Catholics and Protestants but clarified the Catholic Church's position on significant areas of doctrine, brought moderate reform to the abuses of power, and directly opposed the Protestant Reformation.

- Trent produced a worship liturgy known as the Roman missal.

- *Sola Scriptura*: Latin term meaning that the Scriptures are the sole necessary and sufficient source of our theology

- Pluralism: holding office in more than one location as a bishop

- Conciliarists: those who believe that councils are binding on the whole church, including the pope

Essay Questions

Short

1. What was the Council of Trent's response to the doctrine of *Sola Scriptura*? What was the Council of Trent's view of justification?

2. What was Luther's view of justification?

3. What were some of the impacts of the Protestant Reformation and the Council of Trent?

Long

1. What is the Catholic Church's teaching on justification? How would you respond to a Catholic charge that Protestants do not believe in doing good works? What is the place for good works in the life of a believer?

Quiz

1. Who sparked the Reformation by his opposition to indulgences in 1517, which eventually grew into a larger protest?
   a) Jan Hus
   b) Martin Luther
   c) William Tyndale
   d) John Wycliffe

2. The Council of Trent was held in _____ stages over a period of time.
   a) Two
   b) Three
   c) Four
   d) Five

3. Conciliarists maintained:
   a) The belief in reconciling the various Christians sects throughout the world
   b) The belief that the pope's authority is above councils

c) The belief that councils are binding on the whole church, including the pope

d) The belief that the Spirit spoke through prophets alone

4. Trent did not heal the fracture between Catholics and Protestants but: (p. 101)

a) Clarified the Catholic Church's position on significant areas of doctrine

b) Brought moderate reform to the abuses of power

c) Directly opposed the Protestant Reformation

d) All of the above

5. Pluralism during this time was:

a) Holding office in more than one location as a bishop

b) Maintaining different worldviews at once

c) Allowing for religious diversity within a nation

d) Accepting both councils and the pope as final authorities of faith and practice

6. *Sola Scriptura*, or Scripture alone, means:

a) The Scriptures are to be subordinated to tradition.

b) The Scriptures are the only source of truth.

c) The Scriptures are the sole necessary and sufficient source of our theology.

d) None of the above

7. Martin Luther advocated that we become justified through the:

a) Imputed righteousness of Christ

b) Infused righteousness of Christ

c) Meritorious works of the saints

d) Heavenly intercession of the saints

8. Trent's doctrine of justification believed:

a) God is the one who justifies.

b) Justification is not a one-time event but a life-long work of transformation.

c) A believer cannot be assured of salvation in this life.

d) All of the above

9. The Roman Catholic sacrament of _____ meant that a person had to confess his sins to a priest and do a work of satisfaction.

    a) Baptism
    b) Penance
    c) Confirmation
    d) Eucharist

10. Trent argued deceased saints could be prayed to because:

    a) Christ has one body.
    b) They become angels.
    c) They have their resurrected bodies.
    d) None of the above

CHAPTER 9

Heidelberg Catechism (1563)

You Should Know

- According to Ursinus, the overarching goal of the Heidelberg Catechism is to lead to salvation and comfort.

- The Heidelberg Catechism doctrine of the Lord's Supper was greatly influenced by Calvin's view.

- In the Lutheran doctrine of the Lord's Supper Christ is bodily present.

- In the Zwinglian doctrine of the Lord's Supper Christ is symbolically remembered.

- Transubstantiation: Roman Catholic doctrine that the bread and wine at Mass turn into the actual body and blood of Jesus

- Double predestination: God foreordains some to life (election) and others to punishment (reprobation)

- *Soli Deo Gloria*: Latin term meaning "glory to God alone"

- *Sola Fide*: Latin term meaning "faith alone"

- *Sola Gratia*: Latin term meaning "grace alone"

- *Solus Christus*: Latin term meaning "Christ alone"

Essay Questions

Short

1. What issue led the two Protestant groups of the Zwinglians and the Lutherans to division? What did each side think of that issue?

2. What is the Heidelberg Catechism's approach to the doctrine of predestination? How does the Heidelberg Catechism view the doctrine of the Lord's Supper?

3. How is the Heidelberg Catechism "catholic"? Is this a good approach to theology?

Long

1. What are the five *solas* of the Reformation, and why are they important? Can you defend each of them with Scripture?

Quiz

1. In the Lutheran doctrine of the Lord's Supper, Christ is:

   a) Symbolically remembered
   b) Absent
   c) Bodily present
   d) Spiritually present

2. In the Zwinglian doctrine of the Lord's Supper Christ is:

   a) Bodily present
   b) Symbolically remembered
   c) Spiritually present
   d) Absent

3. The Heidelberg Catechism doctrine of the Lord's Supper was greatly influenced by:

   a) Luther's view
   b) Calvin's view
   c) Zwingli's view
   d) Rome's view

4. The Heidelberg Catechism is composed of _____ questions.

   a) 129
   b) 107
   c) 196
   d) 39

5. The major divisions of the Heidelberg Catechism are:

    a) Old and New Testaments
    b) Roman and Protestant
    c) Grace and mercy
    d) Law and gospel

6. The threefold division of the Heidelberg Catechism, according to Philip Schaff, corresponds to:

    a) God, sin, and man
    b) Faith, hope, and love
    c) Repentance, faith, and love
    d) Father, Son, and Holy Spirit

7. According to Ursinus, the overarching goal of the Heidelberg Catechism is to:

    a) Lead to salvation and comfort
    b) Reconcile Romans and Protestants
    c) Convince people of Anabaptism
    d) Aid German princes in retaining control of their lands

8. What is double predestination?

    a) God predestines his Son to be the author of salvation and men to be saved by him.
    b) God predestines creation and then new creation.
    c) God foreordains some to life (election) and others to punishment (reprobation).
    d) God foreordains both the cause of salvation and the means of salvation.

9. The Heidelberg Catechism rejects what view of the Lord's Supper outright?

    a) Calvin's view
    b) Transubstantiation
    c) Luther's view
    d) None of the above

10. The first question of the Heidelberg Catechism is:

    a) What is the chief end of man?

    b) What does it mean to have no other gods?

    c) What rule hath God given to guide mankind?

    d) What is the only comfort in life and death?

CHAPTER 10

Thirty-nine Articles of Religion (1563)

You Should Know

- The Thirty-nine Articles distanced the Church of England from Anabaptism by affirming infant baptism and church tradition.

- The Thirty-nine Articles follow a visible form of church government similar to Rome.

- The Thirty-nine Articles of Religion were crafted by the Church of England.

- The Thirty-nine Articles' theology of predestination and the Lord's Supper is moderately Calvinistic.

- The Thirty-nine Articles advise to speak about predestination with care.

- Erastianism: the state is over the church

- Henry VIII: broke from Rome because it refused to grant him a marriage annulment; started the Anglican Church; English monarch who was head of the church

- Mary I: Roman Catholic queen who sought to return England back under the control of Roman Catholicism

- Elizabeth I: Protestant queen under whose reign Anglicanism came into its own as a distinct church

- Thomas Cranmer: Archbishop of Canterbury who began to set out Anglican doctrine from a Protestant perspective

Essay Questions

Short

1. In what ways do the Thirty-nine Articles retain certain Roman Catholic distinctions? In what ways do the Thirty-nine Articles bear the marks of Protestantism?

2. What are some results of the Thirty-nine Articles trying to chart a middle path?

3. How do the Thirty-nine Articles present the doctrine of predestination?

Long

1. Given that Anglicanism is one of the most theologically diverse groups of Christians, have the Thirty-nine Articles succeeded or failed? Is it better to have a broad or a narrow confession? Why? Are the early ecumenical creeds broad or narrow in the context of the times they were written in?

Quiz

1. The Thirty-nine Articles of Religion were crafted by the:
    a) Westminster Assembly
    b) Genevan Council
    c) Scottish Presbyterian Church
    d) Church of England

2. What king inadvertently created the Anglican Church?
    a) Richard II
    b) Henry V
    c) Henry VIII
    d) Edward VI

3. For what reason did the king sever the Anglican Church's relationship with Rome?
    a) Rome excommunicated Martin Luther.
    b) Spain discovered the New World before the rest of Europe.

    c) He was disgusted with the power of the clergy over the people.

    d) Rome refused to grant him an annulment to his marriage.

4. At the beginning of the Anglican Church's existence, who was the most significant Protestant Reformer, serving as Archbishop of Canterbury?

    a) John Knox

    b) Nicholas Ridley

    c) William Tyndale

    d) Thomas Cranmer

5. Which queen tried to return the Anglican Church to Roman Catholicism?

    a) Mary I

    b) Mary Queen of the Scots

    c) Elizabeth I

    d) Victoria

6. After this first queen died, who was her half-sister, and which side was she on?

    a) Mary I, Roman Catholicism

    b) Mary Queen of the Scots, Roman Catholicism

    c) Elizabeth I, Protestantism

    d) Victoria, Protestantism

7. The Thirty-nine Articles follow a visible form of church government similar to:

    a) Judaism

    b) Presbyterianism

    c) Geneva

    d) Rome

8. The Thirty-nine Articles' theology of predestination and the Lord's Supper is moderately:

    a) Lutheran

    b) Calvinistic

    c) Anabaptist

    d) Roman Catholic

9. The Thirty-nine Articles distanced the Church of England from Anabaptism by affirming:

- a) Infant baptism and church tradition
- b) Believer's baptism and rationalism
- c) Passivism and triumphalism
- d) Popes and councils

10. Erastianism is the view that:

- a) The church and state are divided.
- b) The church is over the state.
- c) The state is over the church.
- d) The congregations rule over the church.

CHAPTER 11

Westminster Confession of Faith (1646)

You Should Know

- The Westminster Assembly was initially called to revise the Thirty-nine Articles.

- According to Holcomb, the Westminster Confession of Faith's doctrines seek to bring high theology to the everyday believer.

- The Westminster Confession of Faith derives its doctrine of the natures of Christ from Chalcedon.

- The Westminster Confession of Faith derives its doctrine of the Lord's Supper from Calvin's view.

- The Westminster Confession of Faith is thoroughly Calvinistic.

- The Westminster Confession of Faith became the official statement of the Scottish Church.

- Puritans: English churchmen who wanted to reform the church further than where the Anglican church had gone; they desired to see the faith lived out in daily life

- Doctrines of grace: a name for Reformed theology derived from its doctrine of salvation

- Five points of Calvinism: a summary of five central points of the Calvinistic view of salvation

- Reprobation: God foreordains some to everlasting death

Essay Questions

Short

1. What are the five points of Calvinism? Briefly explain each one.

2. What nuances does the Westminster Confession of Faith give to the doctrine of predestination?

3. Why do you think the Westminster Assembly focused so much on the life of a Christian in composing this Confession?

Long

1. What does the Westminster Confession of Faith's utilization of previous creeds teach you about the authors of the confession? How do they model seeking to uphold church tradition according to Scripture? Why do you think they consciously used the same language as prior creeds?

Quiz

1. Which group wanted to reform the Church of England and fought in a civil war?
   a) The Baptists
   b) The Puritans
   c) The Roman Catholics
   d) The Anabaptists

2. The Westminster Assembly was initially called to:
   a) Revise the Thirty-nine Articles
   b) Choose a new king of England
   c) Write the Westminster Confession of Faith
   d) Deliberate on how to unify Rome with the Church of England

3. The Westminster Confession of Faith is thoroughly:
   a) Lutheran
   b) Roman
   c) Arminian
   d) Calvinistic

4. Which of the following is not one of the five classical points of Calvinism?

    a) Unlimited atonement

    b) Perseverance of the saints

    c) Unconditional election

    d) Total depravity

5. What is the doctrine of reprobation?

    a) God ordains some to everlasting life.

    b) Those who join the church will be saved.

    c) God foreordains some to everlasting death.

    d) God preserves his people through their lifelong journey.

6. The Westminster Confession of Faith covers:

    a) Predestination

    b) Scripture

    c) Salvation

    d) The breadth of Christian theology

7. The Westminster Confession of Faith derives its doctrine of the Lord's Supper from:

    a) Luther's view

    b) Calvin's view

    c) Rome's view

    d) Zwingli's view

8. The Westminster Confession of Faith derives its doctrine of the natures of Christ from:

    a) Nestorius

    b) Martin Luther

    c) Chalcedon

    d) Eutyches

9. The Westminster Confession of Faith became the official statement of the:

    a) Anglican Church

    b) Scottish Church

    c) Lutheran Church

    d) French Church

10. Based on the types of concerns the Westminster Assembly had, Reformed theology is also known as:

   a) The doctrines of grace
   b) The doctrines of law
   c) The doctrines of knowledge
   d) The doctrines of the church catholic

CHAPTER 12

Second Vatican Council (1962–65)

You Should Know

- Vatican II gave clergy the freedom to make decisions on their own.

- Vatican II insisted that the laity be allowed to read the Bible.

- According to Holcomb, one of the largest issues of doctrine to be developed at Vatican II was separation of church and state.

- Vatican II allowed for the liturgy to be spoken in common languages.

- The Vatican: capital city of the Papal States and then the last remaining city under the control of the pope

- Paul VI: pope who completed the work of Vatican II

- Pius IX: pope who called the First Vatican Council to strengthen papal control

- John XXIII: Pope who called the Second Vatican Council to bring the Catholic Church into the modern era

- *Aggiornamento*: "updating"; Vatican II's policy of better communicating the traditional doctrines of the Catholic Church to the modern world

- Liberalism: theological movement that attempted to separate the so-called "historical Jesus" from the so-called "mythological Jesus"

Essay Questions:

Short

1. What changes did Vatican II make to Roman liturgy? Why was this significant?

2. What were Vatican II's clarifications about revelation?

3. What were the two main views of what occurred at Vatican II? What do you think happened, and why?

Long

1. What were the three major ideas that guided the Second Vatican Council? Why were they important to its development? How do you think these ideas controlled the agenda at Vatican II, for better or for worse?

Quiz

1. The Second Vatican Council met from which dates?
   - a) 1939–1945
   - b) 1517–1519
   - c) 1962–1965
   - d) 1983–1986

2. Liberalism wanted to separate a _____ from a supposed _____.
   - a) Fledgling church, state-run church
   - b) Historical Jesus, mythological Jesus
   - c) Belief in God, deistic approach
   - d) None of the above

3. In 1871, the pope lost all the Papal States except for: (p. 142)
   - a) Italy
   - b) Sicily
   - c) Cordova
   - d) The Vatican

4. Pope _____ called Vatican I to reassert and establish papal authority over the Catholic Church.

  a) Leo XIII
  b) Pius IX
  c) Gregory the Great
  d) John XXIII

5. Pope _____ called Vatican II to the surprise of everyone around him.

  a) Leo XIII
  b) Pius IX
  c) Gregory the Great
  d) John XXIII

6. According to Holcomb, one of the largest issues of doctrine to be developed at Vatican II was:

  a) The transforming of the elements at the Eucharist
  b) Reconciling Protestants to Catholics
  c) Separation of church and state
  d) The doctrine of justification

7. Vatican II allowed for the liturgy to be spoken:

  a) Only in Latin
  b) Only before priests
  c) In common languages
  d) Apart from faith

8. Vatican II rooted both forms of revelation in:

  a) Scripture
  b) Tradition
  c) The pope
  d) Christ

9. Vatican II gave clergy:

  a) The ability to labor at multiple locations
  b) Freedom to make decisions on their own
  c) An ability to contact the Vatican at will for counsel
  d) The choice to become Protestant

10. Vatican II insisted that the laity:
    a) Are restricted from reading the Bible
    b) May vote for the pope
    c) Be allowed to read the Bible
    d) Could become Protestants

Modern Confessions: Lausanne Covenant (1974) and Chicago Statement on Biblical Inerrancy (1978)

You Should Know

- Lausanne Covenant sought to define the gospel for the sake of missions and emphasized the mission of the church for evangelism and social responsibility.

- Historical-critical readings of Scripture and world evangelism were two challenges that led to the Chicago Statement on Biblical Inerrancy and the Lausanne Covenant, respectively.

- The points unifying the members of the Lausanne Conference included: the lostness of man outside of Christ, salvation is of Christ alone, and the authority of Scripture as the infallible word of God.

- After the so-called Age of Reason, greater attacks came upon Scripture and led many Christian modernists to treat Scriptures as a merely human collection of documents.

- Infallibility: not deliberately misleading or having been misled

- Autographs: the Scriptures written in their very original texts; these no longer exist

- Inerrancy: the doctrine that the Bible is fully truthful in all of its teachings

- Fundamentalism: an extreme conservative response to liberalism which tended to emphasize the divine origin of Scripture at the expense of its human authors

- Inspiration: the view that God breathed out his word through the divine authors and guided them by his Spirit, without working against their unique gifts, to write his perfect word

- Edinburgh Conference: The ecumenical assembly in 1910 which gathered together many churches from around the world to explore global missionary efforts; it failed because it did not set basic parameters of what the church needed to believe

Essay Questions

Short

1. Define and defend inerrancy. Define and defend infallibility.

2. What is liberalism, and why is it dangerous? What is fundamentalism, and what problems can arise from it?

3. What is the difference between evangelism and conversion? Why is this an important distinction?

Long

1. The Lausanne Conference stated that the gospel is not to be restricted to a European cultural context. In what ways can the gospel be shared with different cultures and adapted into their context without compromising its message? Provide potential examples of how this would work.

Quiz

1. What were the two challenges that led to the Chicago Statement on Biblical Inerrancy and the Lausanne Covenant, respectively?
    a) Historical-critical readings of Scripture and world evangelism
    b) The resurgence of Roman Catholicism and the rise of Islam

    c) Merging of denominations and the fading of pastoral identity

    d) Worship wars and evangelistic techniques

2. The church fathers saw Scripture as:

    a) Inspired

    b) Fallible

    c) In error

    d) Equal to tradition

3. After the so-called Age of Reason, greater attacks came upon Scripture and led many Christian modernists to treat the biblical text as:

    a) A merely human collection of documents

    b) Untranslatable

    c) A rule of faith

    d) None of the above

4. Extreme fundamentalists tended to make the Bible's _____ element irrelevant. (p. 154)

    a) Divine

    b) Fallible

    c) Human

    d) Natural

5. Inerrancy is: (p. 155)

    a) The doctrine that the Bible is truthful only in that which pertains to salvation

    b) The doctrine that the Bible is fully truthful in all of its teachings

    c) The doctrine that the Bible was dictated by God to human agents

    d) The doctrine that the Bible is truthful only in what concerns Jesus

6. Strictly speaking, only _____ were inerrant.

    a) The first five books of Scripture

    b) The Gospels

    c) Jesus's words

    d) The original copies of Scripture

7. Infallibility means:

    a) Not deliberately misleading or having been misled
    b) Not mistaken, free from error
    c) Speaking on behalf of God through preaching
    d) Not believing in inerrancy

8. The Lausanne Covenant set out to reach an agreement on the meaning of:

    a) Inerrancy
    b) The gospel
    c) The world
    d) Covenant

9. What was not one of the points unifying the members of the Lausanne Conference?

    a) The lostness of man outside of Christ
    b) Salvation is of Christ alone
    c) Witness to Christ is through deed alone
    d) The authority of Scripture as the infallible Word of God

10. The Lausanne Covenant sought to encourage the church toward:

    a) Social responsibility only
    b) Evangelism only
    c) Evangelism and social responsibility
    d) Reconciliation with Rome

ANSWER KEY

1. A, 2. A, 3. A, 4. C, 5. B, 6. D, 7. A, 8. B, 9. C, 10. C

Notes

Printed in the USA
CPSIA information can be obtained
at www.ICGtesting.com
LVHW090954310723
753738LV00009B/50